BREATHE

It's Your Planet—
Love It!
A Leadership
Journey

Girl Scouts of the USA

Chair,
National Board
of Directors

Connie L. Lindsey

Chief
Executive
Officer

Anna Maria Chávez

Chief
Operating
Officer

Jan Verhage

Vice
President,
Program

Eileen Doyle

girl scouts

PHOTOGRAPHS: Page 23: courtesy of Gordon Hempton; Page 28: by Karen Smul; Pages 32, 38: NASA/courtesy of nasaimages.org; Page 40: by Martin P. Morawski; Page 42: Associated Press; Page 44: courtesy of Spokane Regional Clean Air Agency; Page 46: by Joanna Eldredge Morrissey; Page 55, from top: courtesy of Teens for Planet Earth; ©Greenshoots Communications/Alamy; Pages 58, 59, 61: Sillett & Antoine; Page 87: courtesy of City of Chicago Department of Environment; Pages 100–101: courtesy of Miwa Koizumi; Page 95: courtesy of National Renewable Energy Laboratory; Pages 96–97: by Marina De Luca Fragoso Senra

Page 69: "How's the Air?" quiz provided by Ingersoll Rand, a world leader in building systems and services committed to energy efficiency and clean air.

The women mentioned in this book are examples of how women have used their voice in the world. This doesn't mean that GSUSA (or you) will agree with everything they have ever done or said.

Text printed on Fedrigoni Cento 40 percent de-inked, post-consumer fibers and 60 percent secondary recycled fibers. Covers printed on Prisma artboard FSC Certified mixed sources.

SENIOR DIRECTOR, PROGRAM RESOURCES: Suzanne Harper

ART DIRECTOR: Douglas Bantz

WRITER: Anne Marie Welsh

CONTRIBUTORS: Amélie Cherlin, Judy Gerstel, Kathleen Sweeney, and Laura Rozenberg

ILLUSTRATORS: Carolyn Gavin, Talitha Shipman, Jenn Ski, Otto Steininger, and Hannah Stouffer

DESIGNER: Alexander Isley Inc.

EXECUTIVE EDITOR, JOURNEYS: Laura Tuchman

MANAGER, OPERATIONS: Sharon Kaplan

MANAGER, PROGRAM DESIGN: Sarah Micklem

Breathe

an aerial view

There's more going on with air in your life than you might imagine. So fly around. Dip here and there. No need to toe a straight line in this air!

You might live 40 days without food and three days without water. But you'll only last about eight minutes without air.

Come on in and Breathe awhile

Air is essential—to you and the planet. You and air is really the story of you and your five senses, and everyone else on the planet and their five senses. *Breathe* is a journey to air it up in every way imaginable, using all your senses—sight, sound, taste, touch, and smell.

And you'll become more alert to how you can support what you hold dear. You'll also affirm all that you do, as an heir apparent—of air and all of Earth's precious resources. That may even include saving some cents.

You'll make some space for yourself— some time to just breathe and some time to float on air with your friends. *Breathe* will give you a break from all the daily drama-rama.

As you start *Breathe*-ing, you'll also start finding and lifting off with your very own flair. You'll get a clear sense of who you are right now, and maybe even start to prepare for who you will become! You'll find ways to be more aware of what you do best, and what you value.

Breathe *is about your sense of air and your flair for air—air for the planet and airspace for you. Get ready to take flight. With Breathe, you'll be flying and floating into some amazing new life adventures.*

Air is the lung power in a song, the wind in the trees, the pressure in a tire.

Air makes a great cushion, a comfy raft. It puts the hover in a hovercraft.

When the wind musses your h**air** or turns a giant windmill, that's **air** power in action.

Air creates the lift and the currents on which birds, planes, and, yes, even superheroes fly!

Air puts the rise in bread dough and air dries your clothes. Air cools you and air can keep you warm.

What will you do for **air**?

Air floats through all your senses

You may feel a blast of hot air during a heat wave ... or the sting of cold air on a frigid winter day.

You may smell foul fumes from an idling bus or from the sour stench of sweaty gym clothes ... or even from nasty cleaning supplies.

You may cover your ears at shrill sirens and screeching brakes ... you may be bombarded with billboards that practically scream ... or face smoky air so thick you can actually taste it.

Air It Out

Where are you sitting right now? Take a breath. What do you smell? Is it good or bad? What would you like to smell? What's your favorite indoor smell?

If you're inside, open a window and take a breath. What do you smell? Good or bad? What's your favorite outdoor smell? How does it make you feel?

Sometimes there's good air in you...

You're clearheaded and no challenge seems too big.

Sometimes you're so lighthearted, you practically float on air. You face the world and everyone in it in a carefree way.

Don't forget to eat a pear.

Tastes quite fine with a slice of Gruyère.

EMBRACE YOUR FLAIR

Seize those moments when you feel strongest and most yourself. Try to have more of them. How can you do that?

_____

_____

_____

_____

_____

_____

...and sometimes there's bad air around you

There are days when conflict is in the air. You've bottled up too many feelings and they come blasting out like so much hot, heavy air.

You may feel stuck in the same stale circle of air, maybe the same circle of friends. You wish you could break out—and just air it all out.

Need Some SPACE?

STOP and take notice of the air around you—your friends, family, relationships.

Do things feel fine? If not, what needs improvement?

_____

_____

_____

For tough challenges and big changes, who could you reach out to or team up with to clear the air? Need some tips? Sample *aMAZE*, a leadership journey about making more peace in the world, one relationship at a time.

Check in on your air space, and all your thoughts about it, throughout this journey. And take advantage of all of the journey's breathing room moments. Just look for the Need Some Space, Air It Out, and Cut the Noise suggestions. They're designed especially for you!

Fresh air is your great friend...
Open all your windows as often as you can.

—*How Girls Can Help Their Country: Handbook for Girl Scouts, 1913*

Flowing
Toward Three Rewarding Awards!

Along this journey, you have the opportunity to earn three awards: AWARE, ALERT, and AFFIRM. Earning them will engage you in supporting and nourishing the air of Planet Earth while supporting and nourishing your abilities as a leader, one who is aware, alert, and able to affirm all she does. So look over the lofty award tracker in the back of this book. Check out the flow of these awards (their airy beauty!) and all their potential benefits to you. You'll notice this icon throughout the journey:

It will key you in to various award steps and challenges and examples of possible ways to earn your awards.

PREPARE!
(Hear the Air in There?)

Being ready for any challenge is a quality that unites Girl Scouts. In fact, "Be Prepared" has always been the Girl Scout motto. Girl Scouts were expected to be prepared "for any old thing" that came at them. As they grew, they would be productive world citizens who could face any challenge.

As a Cadette, you probably want to be prepared for the future—for high school and life after high school. Now is a great time to open your mind to all the possible ways you can develop and use your unique flair.

Imagine designing a product that would help people and Earth. You might invent a way to power a kitchen or turn on a light with just a quick blow of breath on a switch. Keep a wide-open mind! Observe all the exciting work that is starting up as the world goes green.

Check out all the women featured in *Breathe* and their awe- (and air-) inspiring careers. Along your journey, take time to meet some women in your region, too, especially those who know something about air! Some may be your air experts. Some may offer new insights into air careers. Maybe a local chef creates recipes from food grown in your local air? What do staff at local yoga studios know about breathing—and running a business? Maybe you can find an entrepreneur who makes fragrant natural products or an artist who creates with recycled materials. Or locate some engineers in your area. What do they do? Who is designing the latest energy-saving gadget or gizmo?

Prepare some questions to get the conversation started. Listen carefully and see where the conversation goes and what else you might find yourself curious about asking.

Beware: It's generally useful to avoid questions that result in simple Yes or No responses. "What do you like about your job?" will likely get you better results than "Do you like your job?"

When exploring air issues with experts (as you go after your AWARE award, for example!), you could start with an introductory line like:

I am exploring issues that relate to improving the environment with a special focus on air. So I am trying to learn as much as I can about air from as many different angles as possible. You are a

_____

(whatever the person does/is an expert in)

So I am wondering what you think about a few things and what people are doing about them.

Then you might ask:

What are your concerns related to ... (think of an issue covered in this book, or maybe in the news)?

What examples of air issues are you aware of in this state/region?

What do you find interesting about the science of air related to your work in (yoga, parasailing, or ...)?

What do you do in your work/volunteer/advocacy role to care for air and Earth?

What do you wish more people knew about air?

You might also find out who this person knows—you might want to know them, too! That's how you build a network.

So you might say,

Once I choose an air issue, I want to build a network of interested people—an Air Care Team (one that can ACT!). Can you suggest people I might reach out to? Would you be interested?

To learn more about specific air-related careers, you might ask:

What is a typical workday like for you?

What challenges or projects are you working on right now?

What skills did you need to learn to do what you do?

What personal qualities do you need to be successful in this work?

What do you like about your work?

What do you wish you didn't have to do?

If you were starting over, would you study or get into something different?

What? Why?

Prepare even more: Practice some of your questions on adults in your life. How much do you really know about what they do?

As you journey through Breathe, *and life, be prepared by keeping some little notes, just for yourself, about all the interesting career possibilities for which you might achieve liftoff!*

The possibilities are limitless, for your future and for that of the air.

Aware

GS

compare AIR

your personal air log

Date:

Observation:

Date:

Observation:

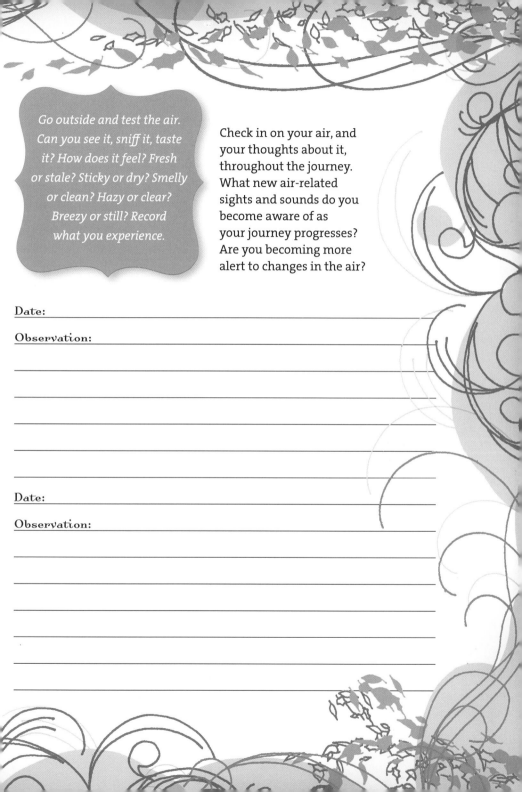

Go outside and test the air. Can you see it, sniff it, taste it? How does it feel? Fresh or stale? Sticky or dry? Smelly or clean? Hazy or clear? Breezy or still? Record what you experience.

Check in on your air, and your thoughts about it, throughout the journey. What new air-related sights and sounds do you become aware of as your journey progresses? Are you becoming more alert to changes in the air?

Date:

Observation:

Date:

Observation:

The Sound of Silence

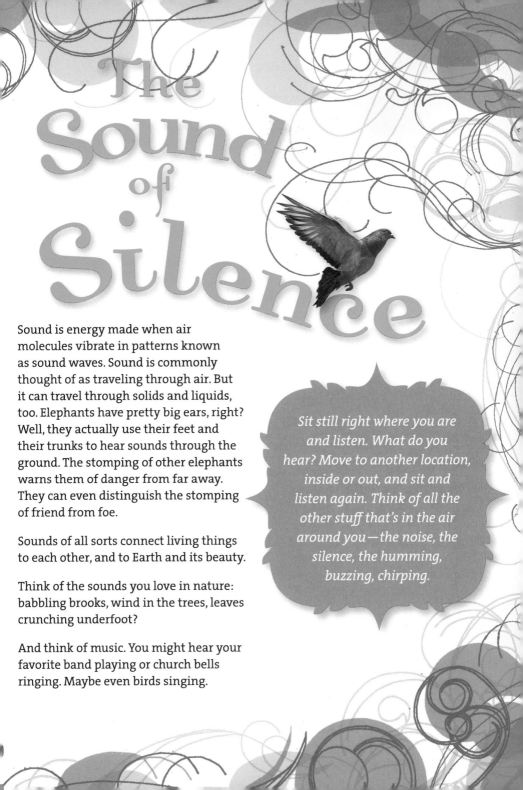

Sound is energy made when air molecules vibrate in patterns known as sound waves. Sound is commonly thought of as traveling through air. But it can travel through solids and liquids, too. Elephants have pretty big ears, right? Well, they actually use their feet and their trunks to hear sounds through the ground. The stomping of other elephants warns them of danger from far away. They can even distinguish the stomping of friend from foe.

Sounds of all sorts connect living things to each other, and to Earth and its beauty.

Think of the sounds you love in nature: babbling brooks, wind in the trees, leaves crunching underfoot?

And think of music. You might hear your favorite band playing or church bells ringing. Maybe even birds singing.

Sit still right where you are and listen. What do you hear? Move to another location, inside or out, and sit and listen again. Think of all the other stuff that's in the air around you—the noise, the silence, the humming, buzzing, chirping.

Some sounds aren't so lovely though. From where you're sitting, do you hear car alarms and air-compression brakes (there's air again!), tires on pavement, blaring horns, sirens in the street, helicopters overhead? Does booming music hit you in the chest before you hear it in your ears? How about the rat-a-tat-tat of a jackhammer? What else?

Maybe your ear is drifting to a TV, radio, MP3s on high. Do you hear a phone ringing or bleeping? Is your computer pinging with IMs and emails?

Yes, we love our high-tech gadgets. But do they separate us from our true connection to nature? Are gadgets why we sometimes get lazy about caring for air and for Earth?

You belong to the most digitally connected generation in human history. How many gadgets buzz or jingle or vibrate through your life? Take a minute and think of all the sounds and sights vying for your attention:

- Cell phones
- Instant messages
- School bells and buzzers
- Videos
- Emails
- Tweets
- Facebook messages
- Texts
- Voice mails
- Alarm clocks
- Robocalls from school
- Reminder alarms

Can you name a minus for each plus? Which can't you live without? Which could you do without?

_____

_____

_____

THINK LIKE AN ENGINEER!

What gadget do you want that hasn't yet been invented?

Engineers design things. What might you like to design someday?

NASA and Noise

When you're riding in a car, do you often feel the vibration of the road, and the constant roar of tires on pavement? Sometimes that roar is so loud you can't hear what other passengers are saying. Well, scientists at the National Aeronautics and Space Administration have invented a material that can quiet even the roar of helicopter blades. Macro-Fiber Composite may be used to minimize noise and vibration in cars, too. Now, that would make for one sweet ride! What else could you use it for?

Music to Your Ears?

Sound is measured in decibels (dB), which describe the intensity of the sound in the human ear. That intensity is the pressure of sound waves against your eardrum. Sound can be a pleasure or a pain. Loud music, for example, can be thrilling to one person and a torment to another.

So finding the right balance of sound in your life is important—to your health and well-being. How loud is too loud?

The answer depends on lots of things, like:

- How often you hear the sounds
- How long the loud sounds last
- Your personal response to loud sounds

Can you rank these sounds in order from softest to loudest?

- Rock concert
- Ambulance siren
- Rustle of leaves
- Quiet conversation
- Mosquito buzzing
- Refrigerator humming
- Loud conversation
- Subway train
- Cranked-up home music
- Car horns
- Gunshot or firecracker
- Space rocket on takeoff
- Chain saw

Prolonged exposure to any sound louder than 85 decibels puts you at risk of gradual hearing loss, according to the National Institute on Deafness and Other Communication Disorders. The institute recommends never exposing yourself to sounds above 100 decibels for more than 15 minutes. And the Occupational Safety and Health Administration recommends serious earplugs for workers using chain saws and other high-decibel equipment.

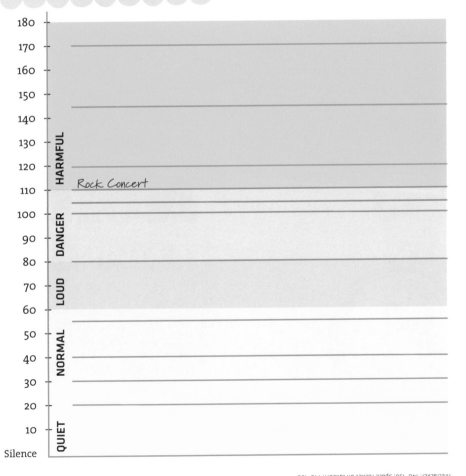

Answers: Rustle of leaves: 20; Quiet conversation: 30-50; Mosquito buzzing: 40; Refrigerator humming: 40; Loud conversation: 50-60; Subway train: 100; Cranked-up home music: 105; Car horns: 110; Chain saw: 110; Rock concert: 110; Ambulance siren: 120; Gunshot or firecracker: 140-150; Space rocket on takeoff: 140-190

When exactly noise becomes noise pollution is hard to define. In the simplest sense, noise pollution is unwelcome noise floating through your air—unwelcome noise that causes stress. Stress can take the form of annoyance, fright, anger, sleeplessness, or a painful ringing in the ears. When have you had some of these reactions to noise?

Noise pollution goes away as soon as the noise stops. But you may still have to deal with the frazzle of frayed nerves.

It's hard to measure how much noise can come into your world before it becomes truly harmful. But for sure, loud noises are a major cause of hearing loss. Baby boomers, the first generation to be raised on rock 'n' roll, are facing more hearing loss at an earlier age than their parents ever did. During the last two decades, hearing loss went up 26 percent for the baby boom generation, which was born from 1946 to 1964. And for people 18–44, hearing loss rose 18 percent. Loud music, whether heard at concerts or through headphones, takes much of the blame.

Have you ever heard music leaking out of someone's headphones? If you can hear it, imagine how loud it is for the person wearing the headphones!

Noise vs. Noise Pollution

So turn down the volume! Of course, sometimes that's tough to do. We tend to raise the volume of our music to rise above the background noise all around us. That sound-noise relationship is known as the signal-to-noise ratio. Our desired signal, our music, must rise above the noise of the world.

Silence=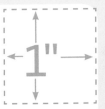

People who meditate try to find a zone of silence where they can feel themselves living fully in the present moment. An independent conservation project called One Square Inch of Silence wants a lot of people to experience that kind of moment—in the quietest place in the United States. This square-inch spot is in the Hoh Rain Forest of Washington state's Olympic National Park, one of the most pristine ecosystems in the lower 48 states. It's a two-hour hike from a visitors' center parking lot.

The point of the project? Preserving this spot of silence will benefit miles of surrounding wilderness. When the silence is broken, offenders are presented with an audio CD of the park's natural soundscape being interrupted by noise.

Check Your Noise Level!

What noise do you make? Think you don't make any? Get AWARE! Get attuned! Learn about your noises big and small. Whose airspace are you invading? Your friends'? Your family's? Neighbors'? Ask around. What can you learn?

Ever tried to give up all your high-tech gadgets for a day, a weekend, a week? What would happen? Try it and find out!

You may be surprised at how nice it can be to create some silent spaces. And think about all the ways you can communicate without making noise: sign language, a knowing glance, a hand-written note. Any others?

Savor the Silence

Have you heard the sound of silence? The zero-decibel kind, when you can actually hear nothing in the air.

Take a deep breath and imagine silence. How about a whole evening of silence? No cell phone, no email, no texting, no iPod. Could you stand it? Just you, some reading, writing, or artwork, and silence all around. Maybe even some daydreams, some wonder, and some special scents. Lavender? Lemon? Mint? Is silence possible in your life? Give it a try.

Impossible? Then try paying attention to all the sounds you like and don't like. Which sounds give you pleasure? Which bother your ears or distract you from things you'd rather be doing? You may be so attuned to them that you're not even aware of their impact on you. Keep track for a week.

Do some sounds make you feel one way on one day and a different way on another?

_____

_____

_____

_____

Now, how might you turn this into a full ALERT? How can you cut down on painful noises (traffic, leaf blowers, sirens) that distract you and your classmates at school or keep you from getting a good night's sleep? Or how can you just create some silence so you can be more aware of your own feelings, or more aware of nature? Most cities have noise ordinances and hotlines for reporting big offenders. What can be done about smaller ones?

What are the policies in your town? How are they enforced? Get your school, neighborhood, or city to commit to reducing noise that impacts everyone's health. Invite your school to create a Silent Sliver each day or week. A strong ALERT might even lead to policy changes, like a stronger anti-noise ordinance. Afterward, you'll definitely be able to AFFIRM the change you set in motion!

Shhh! Can't You See the Quiet Sign?

Girl Scouts have long used a quiet sign to end the murmur of a crowd. The sign is made by holding up your right hand with all fingers extended. Then each person in the audience joins in and holds up her hand, too. The sign is a reminder of the original Fifth Law of Girl Scouting: A Girl Scout is courteous. It uses sight, not sound, for silence!

How About a Media-Manners Manual?

Are cell phones, personal music players, and text messages a constant distraction in your life? Brainstorm an etiquette manual. Start by thinking of what you appreciate about considerate and sensitive media users. Then think about the media-related impoliteness around you. Get **AWARE**!

Do you find loud cell phones and loud cell phone talkers in restaurants, on buses, in workplaces?

_____

What's the craziest personal conversation you've overheard?

_____

_____

_____

How horrified do you think the loud talker would be if she realized exactly what you overheard?

_____

Come up with ways that allow everyone to stay connected—yet respect others and are considerate, too. That's living the Girl Scout Law!

How can you ALERT others?

What new gadgets and gadget modes can eliminate the inconsiderateness?

How can you harness the power of silence as you spread it? AFFIRM your actions!

Here are five ways to secure some quiet breathing room for

YOURSELF!

Need
Some Space?

Light a candle and just sit and breathe as you watch the flame flicker in the moving air.

Lie in the grass and look up—at the clouds, the trees, the rooftops, whatever's in the air.

Make yourself a soothing cup of tea. Watch the steam rise into the air as you sip.

Find a poem, a quote, a song, or any piece of writing that inspires you. Sit quietly and read it. Think about the words. Say them to the air.

Wherever you are, close your eyes and imagine a beautiful place you know. Put yourself there. Feel its air.

Maggie Jackson
Dissecting Distraction

Have you ever made mistakes because you were trying to do too many things at once? Is it hard for you to find a quiet moment just to think or take a breather? Does it sometimes annoy you that friends or family seem distracted when you're talking to them? Is there just too much noise going on?

Journalist and author Maggie Jackson has explored the impact of technology on how people live, beginning with the invention of—not the Internet—the telegraph! She has followed these changes right up to our digital age with its instant messages, virtual-reality games, and cyber chat rooms.

"I wanted to write about how technology was changing people—the broad social issue," Jackson says. "I've always been interested in that."

> *"My favorite places for working without distractions are any library and, yes, the beautiful refuge of the New York Public Library's 42nd Street branch. For quiet fun, I love the beaches of Rhode Island or almost any museum in the world."*

She realized that this age of high-speed connections, multitasking, and media overload was "undermining our powers of attention."

Jackson was born and raised in Sharon, Massachusetts, a rural town outside Boston. She recalls her hometown as "a sleepy place, with no stoplights and a general store."

Growing up near a lake, Jackson had a lot of freedom to bike around with friends and play in the woods. That love of nature has stayed with her.

"Just as we are working toward a green Earth," Jackson once wrote, "we can find ways to create what I like to call 'planet focus' ... a revaluing and cultivating of the art of attention."

Achieving Focus: A Mind-Muscle Exercise

All kinds of people, even executives at big corporations, find it hard to cope with interruptions and distractions. They want to unclutter their minds and focus on creative thinking and productive work.

Focus, says Maggie Jackson, is like the flashlight of your mind. It's what you need to do homework efficiently or to listen closely to a friend. Here are her tips for getting focused:

Set the stage. The right conditions can help you focus. So choose your space and then clear it. Get rid of any distractions, even that note from your current crush.

Silence all your gadgets. Then focus on what you need to do. If your mind drifts to other thoughts, write them down. But put them where they won't distract you. How about stickies on the back of your chair?

Pull back. If you get distracted, just flex your mental muscle! Your brain has neural pathways that you can develop, just like physical muscles, to pull yourself back to the task at hand. If you don't pull back, your mind will be "ever drifting" and you'll become "interruption-driven." That's no way to clear the air!

A stronger focus means more time for fun—and possibly better friendships, because you'll be a better listener.

When a friend is only half paying attention to you, how about trying an "I" statement? You might say something like, "I feel

_____

when you're listening to music, watching TV, and trying to talk to me at the same time."

Think about how it feels when someone you're trying to talk to answers cell phone calls or keeps her earbuds in, rockin' to the music and missing half of what you say. Maggie Jackson calls this "split focus." At home, school, or the office, "split focus" sends a message: "You aren't worth my time."

When have *you* been the one allowing something to distract you, so that you are not fully listening to a friend or family member?

Now, switch gears! Can you think of times when multitasking might be a good or necessary thing?

_____

_____

_____

_____

The Multitasking Life, by the Numbers

5–8 The number of media used by one-third of 14- to 21-year-olds while doing homework.

6 The number of hours of nonprint media U.S. teenagers experience each day (often using more than one screen, dial, or channel at a time).

24 Where U.S. 15-year-olds rank, among 29 developed nations, in problem-solving skills involving analytic reasoning.

25 The percent of restaurant meals now ordered from a car (up from 15 percent in 1988).

33 The percentage of workers who say they are so overloaded they don't have time to reflect on or process the work they do.

28 The percent of a worker's day consumed by interruptions and the requisite recovery time.

25–30 The number of minutes it takes for a worker to resume focus on a task after a distraction or disruption of attention.

IN TOUCH WITH AIR

Air is the everyday name for Earth's atmosphere, a layer of gases that rises and falls and circulates above Earth's surface, creating weather patterns and influencing the climate.

Earth's atmosphere absorbs the sun's hot, ultraviolet rays and helps reduce temperature extremes between night and day. Essentially, it serves as a "blanket" for Earth, protecting **life** on the planet.

Mostly, the atmosphere consists of **nitrogen** (N₂, 78 percent) and **oxygen** (O₂, just over 20 percent). The other 2 percent comes from various gases, best known as greenhouse gases. They trap heat and keep just enough of it close to Earth's surface to sustain life.

Over time, those **greenhouse gases** have been on the rise, leading to a gradual warming of Earth's temperatures, both on land and in the oceans. This temperature rise, and the various climate changes resulting from it, is known as global warming or climate change.

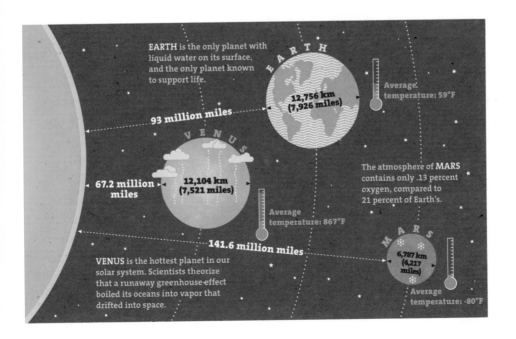

EARTH is the only planet with liquid water on its surface, and the only planet known to support life.

E A R T H

12,756 km (7,926 miles)

Average temperature: 59°F

93 million miles

V E N U S

12,104 km (7,521 miles)

67.2 million miles

The atmosphere of MARS contains only .13 percent oxygen, compared to 21 percent of Earth's.

Average temperature: 867°F

141.6 million miles

M A R S

6,787 km (4,217 miles)

VENUS is the hottest planet in our solar system. Scientists theorize that a runaway greenhouse effect boiled its oceans into vapor that drifted into space.

Average temperature: -80°F

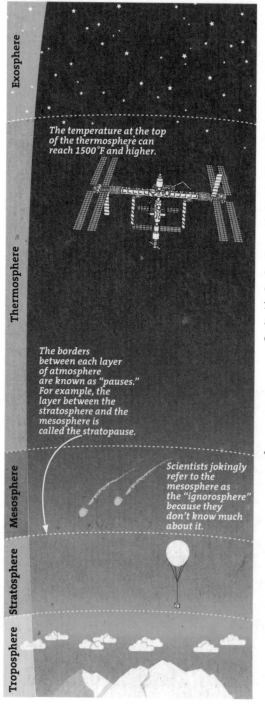

Exosphere

The temperature at the top of the thermosphere can reach 1500°F and higher.

Thermosphere

The borders between each layer of atmosphere are known as "pauses." For example, the layer between the stratosphere and the mesosphere is called the stratopause.

Mesosphere

Scientists jokingly refer to the mesosphere as the "ignorosphere" because they don't know much about it.

Stratosphere

Troposphere

Global warming and climate change have long been hot topics. As some scientists gathered evidence that global warming was real and caused by carbon dioxide (CO_2) emissions, a competing group denied that global warming was even happening. Now, after 20 years of study, the Intergovernmental Panel on Climate Change has concluded that the evidence of global warming and its link to fossil fuel emissions is "unequivocal."

Global warming is more than just small degree shifts in temperatures. Some climate changes, such as unpredictable floods and droughts, and more intense and more frequent hurricanes, are so extreme they are called global weirding.

Armchair quarterback and armchair warrior—you've probably heard of these terms, right? Well, a real leader doesn't just watch from the comfort of a cushy (there's air again!) chair. She gets in the thick of things, maybe even becomes a chairperson to make sure the job gets done. You don't have to be clairvoyant to do that!

THE FOSSIL in FOSSIL FUELS

Coal, oil, and natural gas formed deep in the ground long before the dinosaurs lived on Earth. Coal began as swamp plants that died and became buried under the water of the swamp. Squeezed by heat and pressure, the plant material slowly changed to coal. Oil and natural gas formed from decomposing prehistoric algae and microscopic organisms deep below Earth's surface.

It took hundreds of millions of years for these fossil fuels to form. Today, humans are releasing carbon back into the atmosphere by burning the fuels and creating CO_2 at an alarming rate. A leading cause of air pollution is the burning of fossil fuels—oil, coal, and natural gas—the very fuels that are used daily to generate electricity, heat buildings, or power transportation vehicles.

WHAT'S in AIR?

The ancient Greeks believed air, along with earth, water, and fire, was one of four elements basic to everything on Earth. Native Americans had similar early theories. So did the Japanese. It wasn't until the 1600s that chemists began to suspect that air was not one element but several. In the 1700s and 1800s, scientists were able to isolate various components of air, including carbon dioxide, hydrogen, and oxygen. Argon was not isolated until 1894.

N$_2$

Nitrogen 78.084% There's plenty of nitrogen in the air, but neither plants nor animals can absorb it that way. It first needs to be broken down in the soil into other forms.

Ar

Argon 0.934%
Argon does not react with other elements so it is often used like a protective coating. A glass case filled with argon keeps the original Declaration of Independence in good condition.

O$_2$

Oxygen 20.9476%
Earth is the only planet with enough oxygen to support life.

CO$_2$

Carbon Dioxide 0.0314%
Carbon dioxide makes sodas fizz and bread dough rise.

Ne

Neon 0.001818%
You can thank neon for all the colorful flickering signs in store windows.

Hydrogen 0.00005%

Two atoms of hydrogen (H) together with one atom of oxygen (O) make up H_2O, otherwise known as good old water. A process called electrolysis breaks water back down into hydrogen and oxygen. The hydrogen can then be used to power a car.

Krypton 0.000114%

Don't confuse krypton with Superman's fictional home! The real krypton is used in fluorescent lights.

Methane 0.0002%

Methane is a greenhouse gas. The more greenhouse gases in the atmosphere, the hotter the planet gets, which can cause all kinds of environmental problems. Cows are one of the biggest producers of methane gas—through burping!

Xenon 0.0000087%

Xenon comes from the Greek word for stranger. Xenon is used to power spaceships; it can also be used to put people to sleep during surgery.

Helium 0.000524%

Ever sucked the air out of a balloon and then gone around talking in a squeaky voice? Helium is the gas that does that.

A *World* Working Together for AIR

O zone, or O$_3$, is a natural gas made of three oxygen molecules bonded together. The bad ozone is close to the planet's surface and contributes to smog. But high in the stratosphere, between 50,000 to 115,000 feet above Earth's surface, a layer of good ozone protects life by absorbing some of the sun's powerful ultraviolet rays. This ozone forms a thin protective shield for Earth's atmosphere.

In the 1980s, clues were found that this ozone layer was thinning, allowing more UV radiation to reach Earth's surface.

Then it was discovered that gases called chlorofluorocarbons (CFCs) were carried by winds into the stratosphere. CFCs are made up of chlorine, fluorine, hydrogen, and carbon. When they break down, they release chlorine, which breaks apart the ozone. CFCs were in coolants, foam, and soaps. Other ozone-eating chemicals were in pesticides and propellants that put the spritz in fire extinguishers and hairspray. To halt the ozone depletion, countries around the world agreed to stop making and using these chemicals. Now the ozone layer may be on the mend. That'll be an air ALERT with an AFFIRMative ending!

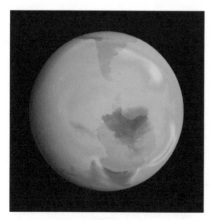

Ozone hole (dark blue), 1979

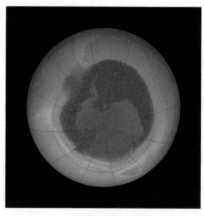

Ozone hole, 2007

Tiny Bird, Big Air Job

The phrase "a canary in a coal mine" means serving as an early warning of an impending crisis. And that's exactly what these petite birds with the airy name used to do. Being sensitive to dangerous gases like methane and carbon monoxide, caged canaries were essential "equipment" for coal miners in the days before mines had ventilation systems, which now spare the birds. As long as their canary sang, the miners knew the air was safe. If the bird fell ill, it was time to evacuate. These days not only do mines have advanced ventilation systems but technologies are being developed to capture the methane from coal mine shafts so that it can be used to produce power or to fill local heating needs.

NASA at Work on Air

By now you know that NASA doesn't just focus on things in outer space. Its scientists have been using satellites to study our home planet's water cycle, weather, ecosystems, and atmosphere—and how climate change is affecting them. That means some NASA employees are focused on what's in our air. In fact, NASA has developed bacterial spore-detection systems to alert pilots to impending danger in air travel on Earth. These systems will be used on journeys to the Moon and Mars, and will eventually detect foreign airborne particles in hotels, apartments, and office buildings here on Earth, too.

B eijing's brown cloud of air pollution made news during the 2008 Summer Olympics, yet it probably seemed far away to most Olympiad viewers. Sitting on the sidelines, though, fascinated and hard at work, were scientists from the Scripps Institute of Oceanography in La Jolla, California. They used the Beijing Summer Olympics as a test case for sampling air pollution, its impact, and the effectiveness of new Chinese government measures to reduce pollution from car traffic and the burning of coal.

Changes in

Yan Feng and Odelle Hadley were on that study team. Feng is an expert on "China transport," the movement of that noxious brown cloud to other places. Hadley is a specialist in measuring soot's impact on snow and climate.

"We have had mathematical models of the transport of black carbon in air for a long time," Feng says. A satellite, for example, can show how long a weather system takes to move the carbon through the world. "But we needed real aircraft measurements to know this for sure," she adds.

A computerized machine called an aethalometer measures black carbon concentrations by using light to scan particles collected in a filter. During the Olympics, the Scripps team leader, Veerabhadran Ramanathan, was on the South Korean island of Jeju, about 500 miles downwind from Beijing and its pollution. There he launched unmanned aerial vehicles (UAVs) containing miniature aethalometers to monitor air quality as high up as 12,000 feet. The UAVs continued to monitor the air after the Olympics ended and the August 2008 restrictions on traffic and coal burning around Beijing were lifted. The scientists also used manned airplanes launched from Edwards Air Force Base in

California. The collected data led the team to conclude that brown clouds of pollution do not disappear harmlessly.

"We used to think of this brown cloud as a regional problem, but now we realize its impact is much greater,"

Mark Kolbe/Getty Images Sport/Getty Images

The word aethalometer comes from the Greek words *aithale*, meaning thick smoke or soot, and *metron*, meaning measure.

the Air

I walked, worked, or played outdoors at least a half hour.

I slept with my window open.

— "Daily Record of Points" in How Girls Can Help Their Country: Handbook for Girl Scouts, 1913

says Ramanathan, who also led a United Nations scientific panel studying the problem. "When we see the smog one day and not the next, it just means it's blown somewhere else."

The team concluded that a lethal mix of soot, smog, and toxic chemicals blots out the sun, harms people's lungs, and is changing weather patterns in many parts of Asia. When it moves across the ocean in higher parts of the atmosphere, it may not impact our health the way it does when traveling over land, but it contributes to global warming, Feng says.

restrictions that were in place during the Games. The rules require private cars to stay off the road one day a week and also cut back significantly on daily use of government vehicles. The restrictions have removed 800,000 cars from the roads, officials there say.

According to a United Nations report, smog blocks from 10 to 25 percent of the sunlight that should reach Beijing's streets. The report also singled out the city of Guangzhou, in southeast China, where soot and dust have dimmed natural light by 20 percent since the 1970s. What's some news about air in your area?

How long does it take for a brown cloud in China to reach southern California? "It depends on certain conditions," Feng says, "but on average it takes about a week. It's a very short time." In fact, she adds, it's roughly the same time it would take for a car to drive the distance—if a car could cross the ocean!

The team also concluded that the brown clouds might be affecting rainfall far from China—in India and Southeast Asia, for example, where monsoon rainfall has been decreasing in recent years. Meanwhile, devastating floods have become a great threat to central China.

After the Olympics, the Chinese government reintroduced some traffic

The Arab scientist al-Kindi wrote the first known work on air pollution in the 9th century AD. Around 1000 AD, al-Tamimi wrote of air pollution in Islamic states and how it related to the weather. His work also covered diseases caused by air pollution.

What Goes Around Comes Around

Ironic, isn't it, how the car, now a major source of pollution, has always been a vehicle of choice for venturing out in the fresh air?

How I wish I was there . . . to give you a little fresh air in "My Motor."

—Juliette "Daisy" Gordon Low, writing home from India in February 1908 to her father, who was ill with the flu

ITCHIER IVY?

Rising levels of CO_2 create more than weather changes. Researchers studied poison ivy between 1999 and 2004 in a forest near Chapel Hill, North Carolina, where high levels of CO_2 were pumped into test plots. The test plots grew more vigorously and produced a more toxic form of urushiol, the resin that causes poison ivy's rash.

Are you now AWARE of bad air and its causes? Get even more AWARE by watching traffic patterns. Most schools have a designated area where buses drop off and wait for students. Ditto for the place where parents and other drivers line up to drop off and wait. But are the buses and cars idling their engines near open classroom windows? Near the gym? Do the buses use diesel fuel? Get AWARE!

Your Air Care Team: Students, teachers, and staff who breathe the exhaust, your school administration, the school district, maybe the block association or your entire town.

Method: You might reach out to influence your principal, school district contracting organization, the local office of the American Lung Association, town or city officials, friends and family. Educate and inspire!

If you can get your Air Care Team excited about having clean, clear air around school and in their classrooms, they may take their excitement home and begin mobilizing others in the community.

You may be able to:
- Propose moving the waiting zones to an alternate location.
- Propose creating "no-idling zones" within a certain distance from school buildings.
- Advocate and model alternative transportation: Feet, scooters, bicycles. Talk up walk-pooling and its fitness benefits.

Think about other buildings too— libraries, places of worship, even the mall or movie theater.

After your ALERT effort, check back. AFFIRM any changes, big or small, and keep your Air Care Team up-to-date.

GET OUT IN THE AIR!

What things do you do (besides breathing!) that require air? Get some friends together and take time for your favorite air activity or adventure. How was the air around you? How did your airing out make you and your friends feel? Did it give you any ideas about air issues in your world?

Windsurf?
Play Frisbee?
Toot a flute?
Blow bubbles?
Ride a bike?
Sing?

Can you imagine being an au pair and taking a pair of toddlers out into the fresh air?

Outdoor Activities

1.
2.
3.

4.
5.
6.

How the air made me feel

1.
2.
3.

4.
5.
6.

Ideas for air issues

1.
2.
3.

4.
5.
6.

LIZ DUFFY ADAMS
playwright for AIR

In a science fiction play she wrote, a pair of teen scavengers named Jelly and Smak roam a smelly, junk-filled Earth. They meet John, who's just arrived from the Moon.

John and most other humans left Earth after wrecking the place with air pollution and consumer waste. They enclosed the Moon so they could pump in oxygen. They call this redesigned moon "Nearth," which stands for New Earth. And just as they made old Earth unfit for humans, they are making the same big mess of things on Nearth.

When John lands on old Earth, he's wearing a thick black protective mask. In fact, some American cyclists stepped off a plane for the 2008 Summer Olympics in Beijing wearing black masks too. They looked uncannily like John! Their coach had told them that Beijing's pollution was so bad they needed to protect themselves if they hoped to win their races. Real life suddenly seemed a lot like Adams's fictional play. She hopes that won't happen again!

L iz Duffy Adams grew up on the edge of a state forest in Massachusetts and spent a lot of time roaming the woods. "It was kind of like a fairy tale, like growing up in a book. It was magical," she says.

Adams is now a playwright who lives in New York City. When she bicycles there, she worries about the air she's breathing.

For Adams, being a playwright is not that different from being a scientist. "Ideally you're asking questions, inspired by something you read or experienced and that interests you. But when you start writing a play, ideas come in the door unplanned. You pay attention to what excites you."

46

Imagine . . .

Being inspired enough by the air around you, good or bad, to write a play or create some other work of art that alerts others. What ideas have come to you unplanned? Any ideas about air? In what ways have your ideas helped you clarify why you would like to alert others about your air cares?

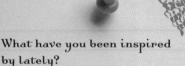

What have you been inspired by lately?

AIR, CHAIRS, STAIRS

To write her plays,

Liz Duffy Adams probably sits a lot—in a ch*air*.

Have you ever noticed
how a ch*air*
basically let's you sit in the *air*?

Where would we be without ch*air*s?

And how about st*air*s?

They let you climb
through the *air*.

What other words do you know with air in them that also let you be in the air? What air, are, aer, and ear (as in pear) words can you have some fun with, turning them into little jingles, raps, poems, or bumper sticker slogans about your cares for air?

GOOD
HAIR
AND BAD *Air*
AN ARTISTIC INTERLUDE

When, in 1967, songwriters James Rado and Gerome Ragni wrote the lyrics to *Hair: The American Tribal Love-Rock Musical*, they pushed air awareness onto the Broadway stage.

Five years earlier, naturalist Rachel Carson inspired the environmental movement with *Silent Spring*, a book that showed how pesticides were killing birds and insects and hurting humans, too. Her work led to the U.S. banning of DDT.

Rado and Ragni took a comic and satiric approach to environmental issues in the air. Their lyrics mentioned sulfur dioxide and carbon monoxide. And they noted that "the air is everywhere." The hippies of *Hair* had audiences all over the world picking up the chorus.

AIRS IN THE *Air!*

In earlier eras, all songs and melodies were called "airs." You may know Bach's famous "Air on a G String" or an air from a Handel opera. Make a playlist of songs about the air and air pollution. Get together with friends and play some of the tunes. What's on your air list? What's your favorite air about air? In what way do these songs inspire you to care about air?

Flair!

That's another word that's really full of air! Rock bands certainly have flair. Sometimes musicians use their flair—and their celebrity—to educate and inspire others. That's a good thing.

You have flair, too! What's your best flair? Like to put together unique outfits? Got a knack for making people laugh? Observing things around you that others rarely notice? Asking just the right question to get to an answer? Designing a solution to a problem? Creating something new? Patience and persistence? You probably have a lot of flair!

Check out the women profiled throughout *Breathe*. Can you see how they're making use of their flair? Think about how they found it. Maybe you have some flair you don't even know about—yet! How can you use your flair to love the planet?

Who are your favorite celebs?

_____

_____

_____

_____

What are they doing for air?

_____

_____

_____

Are they doing enough that you want to put your flair behind theirs?

_____

_____

_____

_____

_____

_____

Éclairs
A Sometimes Treat

Éclairs are full of hot air! And when they cool, they're full of whatever you put in them. Airy as it sounds, éclair actually means "lightning" in French. The secret to this classic puff pastry is that it's cooked once on the stove and once in the oven. Yes, they're rich and they're sweet. Maybe you can try them as just a sometimes treat. And you might put some healthful fruit inside, perhaps even some pear!

INGREDIENTS
1 cup water
½ cup butter
½ teaspoon salt
1 cup all-purpose white flour, sifted
4 eggs, at room temperature

Preheat the oven to 450 degrees and grease a cookie sheet.

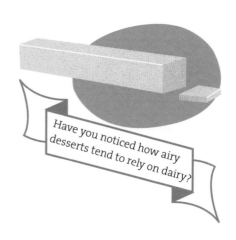

Have you noticed how airy desserts tend to rely on dairy?

In a saucepan, combine the water, butter, and salt; bring to a boil.

Remove the saucepan from the heat and—even though it may seem wrong—add the sifted flour all at once and start stirring. And keep stirring.

The mixture will become a ball of dough. If it doesn't, put the pan very briefly back on the stove and stir again.

Next add the eggs, one at a time. Beat after adding each one until the mixture is shiny—and eventually feels like soft elastic.

To form the éclairs, spread about 3 tablespoons of the mixture into log shapes on the greased cookie sheet; heat makes the pastry puff up with steam and air, so keep the shapes at least 2 inches apart. If you prefer little round cream puffs, just drop big tablespoons of batter on the cookie sheet, again 2 inches apart.

Bake for 15 minutes, then turn the oven down to 350 degrees and bake another 30 minutes until the tops are puffy and the sides feel done.

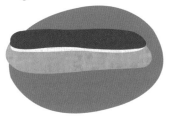

You can fill the éclair shells with a custard or vanilla pudding or some of the whipped creams described below. Just gently cut off the tops with a sharp knife. Spoon in the filling. Replace the top and, if you like, drizzle on chocolate. (Melt chocolate chips in the microwave in short bursts, stirring them now and again with a little milk.)

WHIPPED CREAM FILLING

INGREDIENTS
1 cup very cold heavy cream
1 teaspoon or more sugar
½ teaspoon vanilla

Beat the ingredients together with a rotary or electric beater until the mixture forms soft-to-medium peaks. As it takes in air, it will double in size and become 2 cups. Don't beat beyond the soft peaks stage or the cream will turn into butter!

For variety, add some crushed peppermint sticks or about half a cup of chopped, drained fresh fruit, like peaches, berries, or that pear, to your filling.

Seeing *the* **Forest** *for the* **Trees**

Forests are one way that nature clears the air. They absorb carbon dioxide and release life-giving, mind-clearing oxygen.

Trees also provide shade, reduce the force of winds, and help prevent soil erosion. In cities, they can muffle noise almost as effectively as walls.

Imagine you are walking in a forest and can hear trees, shrubs, and plants breathing. When the sun shines, you might sense a big inhale as trees and plants take in carbon dioxide. In fact, they absorb more than 30 percent of the

carbon dioxide (CO_2) sent into the air by pollutants such as burning coal and oil.

Across North America, Central America, and South America, more than 90 towers in a network called AmeriFlux continuously monitor this daily breathing of forests, crops, and shrubs. AmeriFlux is mostly funded by the U.S. Department of Energy, with some towers paid for by the National Science Foundation and other government agencies.

Beverly Law, a professor at the Oregon State University College of Forestry and the Science Chair of AmeriFlux, is an expert on "biosphere breathing." Since the project began in 1996, she has been using data from the towers to record changes in the amount of CO_2 in the atmosphere.

"We're working as hard and fast as we can to answer some of the big questions about how to mitigate climate change," Law says. "You need long-term observations to really detect trends."

Because emissions travel, similar towers are needed across the globe, not just in the Americas, where Canada alone has at least 20 towers. Europe has more than 100, and China and Japan have monitoring sites, too. Law works with a forest ecologist from each continent to standardize monitoring and analysis methods throughout the world.

Where Have All the *Forests* Gone?

Around the world, the destruction of forests, known as deforestation, has often resulted from clear-cutting, the chopping down of trees without any replanting efforts.

Clear-cutting obviously reduces one of the great benefits of trees: the amount of oxygen they collectively provide. When clear-cutting takes place in old-growth forests, long-established habitats—and the diversity of plant and animal life they supported—disappear, too.

Deforestation also changes the balance of gases in the air. It is considered the third most significant contributor to global warming, behind the burning of coal and oil (by industry, agriculture, and individuals) and methane (released by cows, rice growing, and mining).

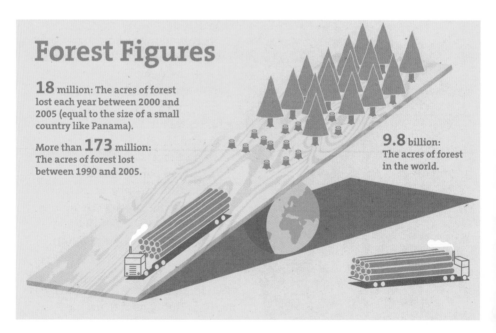

Forest Figures

18 million: The acres of forest lost each year between 2000 and 2005 (equal to the size of a small country like Panama).

More than **173** million: The acres of forest lost between 1990 and 2005.

9.8 billion: The acres of forest in the world.

Tapping into Teak

Above: Teak planting program in Ghana. Left: Teak plantation.

To encourage selective tree cutting rather than clear-cutting, teens in the Volta Region of Ghana in West Africa have planted 15,000 teak trees.

Trees in their region were being cut down by illegal chain-saw operators. As a result, forests were being turned into farms, which increased soil erosion and runoff to streams and lakes. All of this was beginning to reduce local biodiversity.

The teens of the Kubiti Teak Plantation Group received teak seedlings and training from their district's Forestry Department. They established a nursery to raise some of those seedlings and planted others on land secured through Ghana's land tenure system. They've also planted trees around homes, along roads, and at the edges of rivers, and sold some to area farmers.

In Ceiba, a town in eastern **Puerto Rico**, "there are ponds, lagoons, and wetlands," says **Gabriela McCall-Delgado**. So Ceiba is home to an array of birds, many of which winter there during their annual migration.

Gabriela McCall-Delgado:

Realizing that people knew very little about the birds, *las aves*, McCall-Delgado set out to become AWARE and send out an ALERT—by creating the region's first illustrated list of birds. Now a student at Louisiana State University, McCall-Delgado was 13 when she began her project, which earned her both a Girl Scout Gold Award and first prize in Action for Nature's 2006 "International Young Eco-Hero" competition. She photographed birds in streets, parks, lakes, and at the

"I wanted to show people how important it is to care for the environment."

seashore at various times and seasons, then worked with an expert to identify each species. "Some were very common, like herons," she says. "But others were more interesting, like birds that are protected and migratory birds." She identified more than 70 species.

Bringing Birds to the People

A big part of McCall-Delgado's work involved building community support. She had to secure access to restricted parts of the island, which she accomplished by convincing the mayor of Ceiba to obtain a bird-watching permit for her. Her 50-page booklet was distributed to libraries and schools.

To reach even more people, she made a slide show and a computerized puzzle game for elementary school students, as well as an illustrated calendar distributed to visitors by the city of Ceiba. "I wanted to show people how important it is to care for the environment, our beautiful environment," she says.

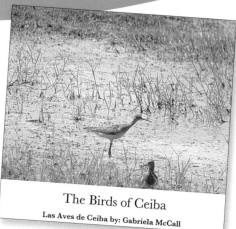

The Birds of Ceiba
Las Aves de Ceiba by: Gabriela McCall

Marie Antoine

LOOKING AT
LICHENS
30
STORIES
UP

From her perch more than 300 feet up in the world's tallest redwoods, Marie Antoine studies lichens and other organisms in their complex aerial ecosystems.

Antoine grew up in a cabin on one of thousands of islands in Lake of the Woods, in Ontario, Canada. "There were lots of trees to climb and rocks to look at. I spent a lot of time climbing up rock faces," Antoine remembers.

While a student at the University of Oregon, she climbed rocks too. The more she climbed, the more she noticed "weird things" growing on the rocks, and on trees and forest floors. Those weird things were lichens.

After Antoine moved to Oregon State University to major in environmental science and botany, she became fascinated by the *Lobaria oregana* lichen, a source of nitrogen in old-growth forests.

To study it, she had to work high in the forest canopies—at Wind River Canopy Crane, a research facility in a forest near Carson, Washington. While swinging in a basket suspended from a crane, she collected samples and conducted experiments in the treetops.

"You are always aware that you are 300 feet up."

Two Great Ways to Share the Air! Have a sleepover on air mattresses or a sleep-out under the stars.

Antoine loved the experience. It led to her giving a talk about her research to other forest biologists. In that audience was a well-known lichenologist and tree expert named Stephen Sillett. He invited Antoine to study in the giant redwoods of northern California.

Antoine's favorite air spot: Trinidad, California

Working high in the redwoods, surrounded by moss, lichens, and fern gardens, Antoine can seldom see the ground 30 or more "stories" below her. But working in Australia in giant eucalyptus trees, with their fewer branches and thinner foliage, "You are always aware that you are 300 feet up," she says.

Antoine now teaches near California's redwoods, at Humboldt State University, and continues her research in forest canopies around the world.

So, how are you lichen this?

"You can breathe fresh, clean air straight off of thousands of miles of Pacific Ocean. I like to think of it as 'ocean breath.'"

LICHENS, NATURE'S *Air* MONITORS

Lichens look like a brightly colored crust growing on rocks and tree trunks. They are actually a symbiosis between fungi and a partner like green algae or a special nitrogen-fixing bacteria. They can grow anywhere: Each lichen is its own miniature ecological community.

Some lichens are pioneers, colonizing spots too harsh for most other organisms to thrive on, such as fresh lava, bare rock, bones, and even glass and rusty metal. Other lichens live only in pristine, undisturbed habitats like old-growth forests.

All lichens get their water and nutrients directly from the air. They act like sponges, sopping up everything that comes their way, including air pollution. So lichens are good indicators of an ecosystem's health. Some lichens are highly sensitive to pollution and can be killed by it. Others are pollution-tolerant. The U.S. Forest Service uses them to monitor air quality by keeping track of which species are growing and where, and how species distributions change over time.

IMAGINE

Working high up in nature—in the trees like Marie Antoine, or maybe on a mountaintop. Can you imagine feeling a gentle breeze up there? Or a big blast from an icy gust? What might you see? What would you choose to study? The next time you and your sister Cadettes get out in the great outdoors, look for some lichens. Where do you see them? What shapes do you find? What in nature fascinates you? How can your fascinations lead you to an air issue worth caring about?

Hares, Mares, Bears! Oh, My!

Sometimes it's nice to have a little fun with words. It can air out your brain! How many airy-sounding animals can you think of?

_____

_____

_____

Get your friends to try too. Maybe include some little kids, and make a game of it.

There's the **polar bear**, who can breathe on land and hold its breath in water. **Mares** gallop, as if flying through the air. **Hares** get all fluffy in the air (and they get named Fluffy, too).

Airedales are very alert but also get distracted a lot (sound familiar?). Prairie dogs come out of their burrows and sniff the air of their prairie home.

Airborne animals count, too, like **monkeys** flying through the air with the greatest of ease.

Get Out in the *Air!*

What policies does your town have in place for green spaces? What new policies and practices might your community need? What could you do now to get the ball rolling? Whom would you ALERT? How would you AFFIRM? What could you do someday in the future if you study urban design, architecture, or landscape architecture?

Permanent Paper Reduction

Deforestation usually involves huge tracts of land. But it can occur on a smaller scale, and in urban areas, too—to create office "parks" or open backyards.

Get AWARE! Take a walk through your community with some Cadette friends. Are any office buildings or new homes being built? Were trees cleared to make way for these buildings? How does it make you feel to see raw earth and concrete where green trees once stood? Were any new trees planted to re-green these areas?

If you're getting AWARE of deforestation and air pollution, use what you know to make the case for keeping forests healthy by reducing the amount of paper your school and its affiliated organizations use.

Start in your own classroom. Have a contest to weigh the amount of paper used each week. Keep weighing and recording the results for a month. Take the effort community-wide. Kick it off with a talk by a forest biologist, Forest Service worker, or arborist. How far can you spread the effort? How can you AFFIRM it?

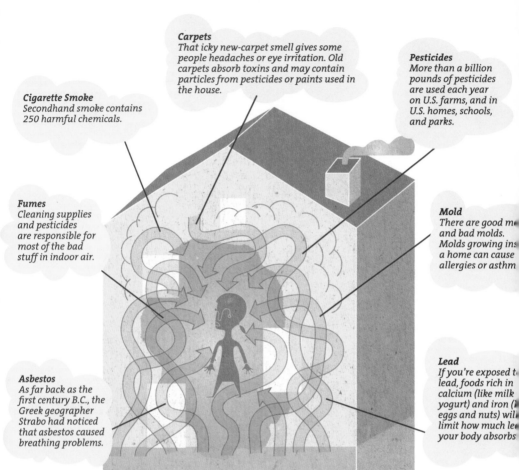

Carpets
That icky new-carpet smell gives some people headaches or eye irritation. Old carpets absorb toxins and may contain particles from pesticides or paints used in the house.

Pesticides
More than a billion pounds of pesticides are used each year on U.S. farms, and in U.S. homes, schools, and parks.

Cigarette Smoke
Secondhand smoke contains 250 harmful chemicals.

Fumes
Cleaning supplies and pesticides are responsible for most of the bad stuff in indoor air.

Mold
There are good m• and bad molds. Molds growing ins• a home can cause allergies or asthm•

Asbestos
As far back as the first century B.C., the Greek geographer Strabo had noticed that asbestos caused breathing problems.

Lead
If you're exposed t• lead, foods rich in calcium (like milk yogurt) and iron (• eggs and nuts) wil• limit how much le• your body absorbs•

What Are You Breathing In?

New paints no longer contain lead, which is bad for your health. But they release volatile organic compounds (VOCs). VOCs can make you feel sick and can trigger allergies and asthma attacks.

Cleaning supplies— the toxic, synthetic, and industrial-strength kind—are a major source of VOCs. Their strong odors irritate the lungs and upper airways just like paint fumes and cigarette smoke.

Reactions to them can be the same as those produced by natural allergens like pollen and cat hair: coughing, wheezing, phlegm, runny noses, watery eyes.

BAD *Air* HURTS *(and Smells!)*

Air is usually free. But when it's polluted, you may be paying for it—with your health. Air pollution–related illnesses are on the rise, especially among young people. A variety of substances and gases in the air, as well as mold and allergens, pose health risks.

The indoor air of classrooms, cafeterias, gyms, locker rooms, and bathrooms can become especially polluted. Why? They have four times the human density of most offices! And if toxic cleaning substances are used in them, those substances can be inhaled, taken in through skin contact, or ingested accidentally.

Making schools greener makes students healthier. That means fewer absences, and more opportunities for learning!

Breathing
ROOM,
PLEASE!

Medical advances in treating illnesses are in the news nearly every day. Yet worldwide rates for asthma have steadily increased, with children under age 5 the hardest hit. People with asthma are sensitive to allergens such as pollen and many other irritants, including cigarette smoke, dust mites, and air pollution.

Nearly **8** percent of the U.S. population, or **24** million people, suffers from asthma.

That's **6** million kids. Childhood rates are nearly **9** percent.

Maybe you have a friend who needs to use an inhaler at times?

What's up with that?

Answer: What's in the AIR

to even tiny amounts of airborne irritants can cause the airways of asthma sufferers to constrict, making it difficult to breathe. Breathing during an asthma attack is often compared to breathing through a straw. That's how small the airways can become.

The Good News:

Ridding the air of irritants can definitely keep asthma attacks under control. The not-so-good news: When it comes to schools, a lot of change may be needed. Check out these numbers:

About **20** percent of the 115,000 schools in the United States have indoor air-quality problems. And nearly one in five Americans, more than **55** million people, spend their days in K–12 schools—not just students and teachers, but administrators, nurses, janitors, and parent volunteers, too.

Of the **48** pesticides most commonly used in schools, the Environmental Protection Agency classifies **22** as possible or probable carcinogens.

Around the globe, more than a billion people rely on wood-burning stoves. According to a study in Nepal, the pollution created by an indoor cooking stove can be compared to smoking **20** packs of cigarettes a day!

What's in Your Air?

Get AWARE! Find out how much particulate matter is in your air. Leave a piece of clear tape sticky side up for a day on your windowsill or desk and in various other locations—outside your front door, inside the door at floor level, at counter level in your kitchen, on top of the refrigerator, and inside your closet.

You might also place a piece of double-sided tape on the handlebars of your bike. Or try the bumper of a car or the edge of a windshield. You could even "wear" the tape on a hat or stick it to your backpack or sleeve. What the tape collects will give you an idea of the particles and dust around you that day.

Then collect all your pieces of tape and place them sticky side down on a white index card or a piece of paper. You can see the larger particles you've collected with your eyes, and you'll see smaller ones with a magnifying glass.

Measure and compare the particles you've collected: Use the same small defined area each time—say, the size of a hole in a piece of notebook paper. Place the hole over the tape, then count the particles.

Now pull back the tape and touch the particles! What do you feel?

How's the *Air?*

These air questions may seem tough, but their answers offer a lot of fascinating facts. See how many answers you know or can figure out.

1. How many allergens find their way into your home every day?

A. 916 million
B. 115 billion
C. 18 trillion
D. 72 trillion

2. Most homes generate about ___ pounds of dust per year for every 1,500 square feet of space.

A. 20 (the weight of 32 boxes of Trefoils)
B. 40 (the weight of 64 boxes of Thin Mints)
C. 60 (the weight of 137 boxes of Tagalongs)
D. 80 (the weight of 160 boxes of Samoas)

3. Since children breathe faster and inhale 50 percent more air per pound of body weight than adults, they ingest anywhere from 50 to 100 milligrams of dust per day, which is 100 times more than adults ingest. This amounts to about a _____ of dust every six weeks.

A. Teaspoon
B. Tablespoon
C. Cup
D. Pint

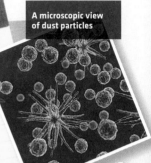

A microscopic view of dust particles

Dust mites on wool

Dr. Dennis Kunkel / Visuals Unlimited / Getty Images

Sniff and Search!

Clean Machine Inventory

*Do the halls in your school ever smell like chemicals? Do the bathrooms have that eye-stinging bleach aroma? How about other buildings in your life? Your community center, town library, or place of worship? And how about your bathroom at home? Get **AWARE**!*

Do a little inventory of what products are in the air around you.

_____

_____

_____

_____

_____

_____

• Talk to your family about what's in the cleaning closet and laundry room. Read the labels. Be sure an adult is with you when you investigate.

• At school or in other community buildings, find out who buys the cleaning supplies. Perhaps it's a contractor. Get permission to find out what cleaners are being used. Or perhaps those in charge of the building can get a list of them for you.

• Research the ingredients. Are any harmful? Can they be replaced with "green" products or by homemade natural alternatives? Think about your school and its classrooms, and the gym and the cafeteria. Which places smell good? Which need freshening?

_____
_____
_____
_____
_____
_____
_____
_____
_____
_____
_____
_____
_____
_____

You might also look into all the plants that help clear the air (see pages 82–83). Could you convince your school to try some fresh approaches? By the way, do  commercial air fresheners cure the stink or simply mask it? Can you find natural alternatives? Whom might you get to expand your Air Care Team? Horticulturalists? Nursery owners?

And you might explore the EPA's Tools for Schools program, which helps schools identify, correct, and prevent indoor air-quality problems. An Indoor Air Quality Action Kit is available to schools at no charge and is co-sponsored by parent, school, and teacher groups, as well as the American Lung Association. Go wide and reach out to the whole school district!

And **AFFIRM** your efforts. **What changes are you seeing? Tell your Air Care Team about them.**

Nature's Alternatives

Vinegar, lemon juice, baking soda

These three staples of your kitchen cupboard may sound like they belong in a cake or salad dressing, but your great-grandparents probably knew they were three of the most effective cleaning products out there.

An open box of baking soda will absorb foul odors anywhere, even those in sweaty sneakers and gym clothes. Vinegar mixed evenly with water is a great cleaner for window glass. And want nicer nails? Rub the tips of your fingers in a lemon quarter, right down to the white inside the rind. Your nails will be cleaner than clean.

Ellen Sandbeck
Ketchup and Olive Oil, Too

Ellen Sandbeck's interest in nontoxic living began in sixth grade, when she attended her first environmental education camp. But the subject really hit home when she was in her 30s and learned she was allergic to chemical fragrances in laundry detergent.

Sandbeck, who lives outside Duluth, Minnesota, is now the author of books on nontoxic gardening, nontoxic cleaning, and nontoxic living. She advises people to avoid toxic and poisonous products. She also encourages a ban on caustic drain cleaners and chlorinated cleansers because the synthetic chemicals they contain can harm you and the planet.

Instead, Sandbeck advocates cleaning with natural products—particularly white vinegar, baking soda, and lemon. But ketchup and olive oil are also the

"If you can eat it, you can safely clean with it"

basics of green cleaning, she says. Ketchup polishes copper. Olive oil is good for hair care. "If you can eat it, you can safely clean with it," she says of the many kitchen products in her arsenal.

73

Cutting through the STATIC

If you're trying to detox your air, and your airspace, you'll find that many products are labeled "green" or "eco-friendly" or "nontoxic" or "environmentally safe." But are they truly green? So much contradictory information is out there, what's a girl to do?

Step back, evaluate competing claims, and decide for yourself.

Don't expect instant results. Give yourself time.

Use your instincts. Would you rely on an ad to learn if a product is worth buying? Remember: Advertising's goal is to lure you in!

Here are a few tips to help you sniff out some more reliable sources of information.

If the extension is **.gov**, that means the U.S. or a state government stands behind the information.

If the extension is **.edu**, that means the information comes from a school or university Web site. Often you can be confident that the information is accurate—unless you are only looking at a student-written paper or blog.

- **For green products,** try Consumer Reports or other consumer magazines or Web sites that aren't owned by the manufacturer trying to sell you a product.

- **For appliances,** the government has an Energy Star rating it gives to energy savers from dishwashers to light bulbs to printers for your computer. Be sure to look for the rating on items you buy and encourage your parents to check for the telltale star on major purchases.

If the extension is **.org**, that means you are looking at a nonprofit organization's Web site. Just be sure that the organization is not the same company that wants to sell you the product you are researching. As the saying goes, buyer beware!

- **Online,** there are some strong signals for reliability. One good way to know if the information has expert backing is to see what extension is at the end of the domain name. An extension is the last two or three letters after the final period (.) in the name of a Web site.

Often when you Google a subject, a Wikipedia entry comes up first. Wikipedia can offer a good start, but it's not enough. Anyone can post information there, including people who don't know much about the subject. Scroll down to the bottom of the page and you'll find a list of sources. Click on those and see if the information matches.

Serious library researchers try to find at least two independent sources to verify the same information. When possible, you should too.

As a society, we all know the ills of smoking. We have health warnings on cigarette packages, anti-smoking programs in schools, and smoking bans in planes, restaurants, offices, and other public places. Yet every day, people still light up.

SO MUCH SMOKE!

Let's focus for now on your air. How much tobacco smoke do you see around you? Are any of your classmates smokers? Why do they do it? What can be done to help them kick the habit?

And why do people even start smoking? Maybe it just seems cool?

List the reasons why you think young people start to smoke. Do they think it's cool? Are they influenced by movies and TV? Are they just curious? Rebellious?

1. _____
2. _____
3. _____
4. _____
5. _____
6. _____

Now, beside each reason write a stronger one that undercuts it. If you wrote, "They think it's cool," you could write, "But it gives you smelly breath and stinky clothes. Not cool!"

Smoke ALERT

Whenever you want to educate and inspire others, facts work best.

1,200 Americans die each day from tobacco use and exposure to secondhand smoke.

Cigarettes can lead to many cancers, especially lung cancer.

A pack of cigarettes usually costs more than $5. So a one-pack-a-day smoker spends over $1,800 a year on her habit. What would you do with $1,800?

Nicotine and other chemicals in tobacco are poisons that can cause heart disease.

Smoking decreases blood circulation, making smokers tired and cranky.

Breathing Better
in
Beverly Hills

In the summer of 2006, best friends Chetana Singh and Wendy Weng, both rising juniors at Beverly Hills High School in California, decided they wanted to do something about smoking. Their fathers were smokers and they wanted to stop teens from being lured into the habit.

They contacted a group called BREATHE LA and learned how critical it is for peers to get involved. "Because cigarettes are legal, some teens don't see the problem," Weng says. "They get addicted to nicotine and don't even know it."

Weng and Singh talked up the idea with three other friends. They asked a faculty member to be their sponsor and then created a club called 4-U-N-I. "We researched what kind of people smoke, why people smoke, the famous people who smoked, and gathered quit-smoking stories," Weng says.

Then the club members planned a series of projects, including a teen-to-teen Quit Tobacco program. To aid their effort, the group produced two animated shorts and public service announcements about the perils of smoking.

"I'm very passionate about film," Weng says. "Visual media is a wonderful way to spread the news because kids are in school all day and they are really tired of being lectured."

Now she and other members of 4-U-N-I are working on a 15-minute documentary highlighting the dangers of smoking. And BREATHE LA is offering the tools of this Quit Tobacco collaboration to other California high schools, with nearby Granada Hills being the first to form a satellite chapter of 4-U-N-I.

And though Weng's father hasn't quit, he smokes much less now and no longer in the house.

Imagine

You have a good friend you'd like to help quit smoking. How would you educate and inspire her?

_____

_____

_____

_____

After Wendy Weng and Chetana Singh understood the health effects of tobacco and the tobacco industry's attempts to influence youth culture, they came up with these peer-friendly ways of influencing others:

Be kind and supportive of friends struggling with a smoking habit or who are tempted to start.

Present hard facts about smoking in an objective, instead of accusatory, way.

Use "I statements" carefully to express your own feelings about the habit.

Use a sense of humor and teen-friendly media to get your message across.

What other ways could you use to educate and inspire peers to quit?

_____

_____

Count Some *Butts*!

U nhealthy as smoking is, it's still possible to have a little fun trying to end it.

Sit on an outdoor bench and count how many drivers passing by are smoking, and how many pedestrians.

Count up the butts you see around your school or in a neighborhood park. Check on a school day and a weekend day. Compare your totals with those of your sister Cadettes.

_____

_____

Did your butt counts vary by day? Why do you think that is?

_____

_____

_____

NO-BUTT ZONES

Get AWARE. Are your town's streets filled with smokers? Do they congregate at entrances to public buildings? How about at your school?

Your Air Care Team: Students, school staff, the medical community, and the local office of the American Lung Association. Ask them to designate no-smoking areas for all to enjoy. Take it up a notch: Are new policies needed to prevent ads in some places or to ban smoking in more public places?

Kickoff ideas: A Smokers Be-W-Air Fair with booths offering various experiments and activities about smoking, including a look at manipulative advertising, what smoking does to your lungs, and a survey on how people feel about friends who smoke.

Carry it forward to your school district or your wider community. AFFIRM it, too! Can you count up fewer butts than when you started?

Need Some Space?

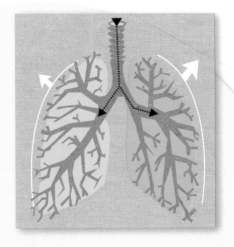

All this smoking talk got you gasping for air? Or maybe you have a headache? Patience can help with mental headaches that disrupt your airspace. Deep breathing can, too. It can even relieve a physical headache. Focusing on breathing relaxes the tension that causes headaches.

Try this: Hold both hands on your ribs and take a deep breath. Feel your ribs expand? Each breath increases the air in your lungs.

The rising air pressure signals your ribs to make more room for your lungs.

Deep breathing is good for your lungs, not to mention your mood! So take a deep breath whenever you can! Try it before you enter your school (as long as no one's smoking there!). Try it on a mountaintop, maybe even a treetop!

Greening with Greenery

One plant will improve the air quality in a room of 10 square yards, with 8- or 9-foot ceilings. That translates to three plants per average classroom. Researching both the amount of natural light in the classrooms and the amount of light various plants need is essential.

Australian Sword fern

English ivy

Areca palm

Weeping fig

Reed palm

Peace lily

Boston fern

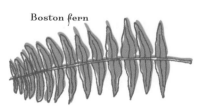

Rubber plant

Janet Craig dracaena

82

Fragrant plants can take the greening one step further. They can help mask cooking and other odors and eliminate the need for air fresheners. Here are some options . . .

String of beads

Scented geranium

Pink jasmine

Gardenia

Wax flower

Hyacinth

How NYC Schools Cleared the *Air*

After the September 2001 attacks on the World Trade Center in New York, air quality was a big concern, particularly in the seven public schools in lower Manhattan that were closed temporarily. Florida nursery growers donated thousands of green plants for the schools, and Horticultural Help, an indoor landscaping business, coordinated their placement. The plants provided fresher air, and an emotional lift for the students.

BE AWARE AS YOU ALERT!

As you observe various advertising techniques being used to get your attention, what can you borrow and adapt for your own use in your air ALERT?

_____

_____

_____

_____

_____

_____

_____

_____

_____

When's the last time you ate air-popped popcorn?

Elevate Your air POWER

Have you ever run or power-walked or climbed stairs until you were panting for air? Well, the more you stay with it, the more you'll increase your endurance, and your lung capacity for air. Exercises that improve lung capacity also improve cardiovascular functioning since the heart, lungs, and circulatory system work together to bring oxygen to all parts of the body.

The more efficiently your body works, the better you'll feel, the healthier you'll be, and the more you can enjoy all the air around you! Plus, you get that "endorphin high" that you hear runners talk about. You'll actually elevate (that's kind of an air word too, right?) your mood and have more energy for everything.

So start simply. Climb one set of stairs each day. Try it for a week. Then take the stairs twice each day. If you're already pretty active, take it up a notch. Got track practice in the afternoon? Try a run in the morning, too! Pretty soon you'll feel how much more energy you have. Try walking around your block, school, Girl Scout meeting place, wherever you go. Soon you'll see it's getting easier and easier to pick up the pace. Before long, you'll be ready for a *Survivor*-style camping/hiking weekend with your GS crew. So start planning!

GREEN ROOFS ROCK!

Most cities

have miles of flat asphalt roofs that can raise the air temperature significantly in summer. Replacing regular roofs with living green roofs can cool temperatures, reduce storm runoff, and provide habitat for wildlife.

In New York, community groups in the Bronx are green-lighting green roofs to alleviate poor air quality and high asthma rates. Some schools have added green rooftop classrooms, where students can garden, draw, write, and breathe a little easier.

Germany leads the way in modern green roof installation, but Scandinavian countries have used turf or sod roofs for centuries to insulate farmhouses. Remember when Laura Ingalls Wilder lived with Ma and Pa in a turf house in Minnesota for a summer? That had a green roof, too!

Amy Norquist plans green roofs all over the world as an environmental designer at Greensulate, a green-roof design firm based in New York and San Francisco. One of her favorite green roofs is on Chicago's City Hall. "Not only has it attracted butterflies and provided habitat for birds," she says, but "studies are showing that folks who look out at the Chicago City Hall roof are actually happier than before the green roof was there."

The program center at Girl Scouts Heart of Michigan has a green roof, too. In fact, the whole building is green. Girls brainstormed with architects and engineers during the building's planning stages. "When we learned about green roofs, we realized that's what we wanted," Jessica Vosburg, 14, recalls.

A green roof is like a mat, explains Ashlyn Katz, and it's planted with sedum, which needs little maintenance. "Sedum is a low-growing plant that's really dense," she says, "so it collects a lot of water and it's kind of rubbery. When it rains, it keeps the rain on the roof." Excess storm water flows directly to the center's five internationally themed gardens down below.

Imagine ...

A green roof on your home or school. How would you design it? What would you like to see growing on it?

The green roof on Chicago's City Hall

Remember, air gives a major lift to cooking—and it's free! Here's an airy confection worth celebrating: meringues. They're as simple to make as 1—2—3. Flavored whipped creams and various fruits (like those offered with the éclair recipe on page 50) are also delicious in meringues.

Meringue Shells

You and a friend could make this together, one beating the egg whites while the other adds the sugar slowly. You'll need some parchment or baking paper to put on a cookie sheet. Then heat the oven to 225 degrees.

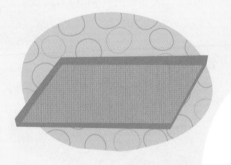

INGREDIENTS

4 egg whites at room temperature
1 teaspoon vanilla
$\frac{1}{8}$ teaspoon cream of tartar
1 cup powdered sugar
a pinch of cinnamon, if you like

DIRECTIONS

Beat the egg whites in a clean bowl until they are foamy.

Beat in the vanilla and cream of tartar.

While continuing to beat the whites, gradually add sugar (and cinnamon, if using) and keep beating until stiff peaks form.

Drop the meringue from a spoon onto the papered cookie sheet. You should have enough for 12 meringues. Use the spoon to hollow out a spot in the center where you will put some whipped cream, fruit, or ice cream.

Place in the preheated oven for about an hour. Then turn off the heat, open the oven door a bit, and let them sit.

Meringue for Pie Topping

You'll need a baked 8- or 9-inch pie shell, filled with lemon or lime filling. Preheat the oven to 350 degrees. For the airy part that will make any pie fancy, you'll need:

2 or 3 egg whites
¼ teaspoon cream of tartar
3 tablespoons granulated sugar
½ teaspoon vanilla

Beat the first three ingredients together until the egg whites form stiff peaks.

Beat in the vanilla.

Spread the mixture on your pie, then bake about 10 minutes or a bit longer until the meringue is just lightly browned.

Feeling the *Wind* at Your Back

ustainable: That word describes the use of materials and energy in a way that allows for people to continue using them without running out. One way of producing electricity sustainably is by using various forms of renewable energy. Renewable energy systems include solar energy and wave energy, and, of course, wind energy. Sustainable wind power may also describe your future career.

Have you seen any of those sleek, slowly turning wind turbines? They generate electricity from a source that will never run out—wind. The wind turns large blades that are connected to an electrical generator. As the magnets in the generator turn past copper wires, they create an electrical field that can be collected and turned into flowing electricity. This is exactly how a motor works, except in reverse. Motors use electricity to turn things, like the cutter on an electric mower or the blades in a blender.

You need *to have enough wind to make it worthwhile to build a wind turbine at a particular location. The tops of ridges and out in the ocean are good places. There is usually a steady strong wind there.*

If you have a place where you have an extra amount of wind power and you want to store the extra energy, you can run an electrolyzer. Electrolyzers use electricity to separate the molecules of water (H_2O) into hydrogen and oxygen gases. The gases can be stored and used for other things. If the wind isn't blowing strongly enough, you can combine the hydrogen and oxygen again in a fuel cell and get what? Electricity! Just as the turbine operates like the reverse of a motor, a fuel cell operates like the reverse of an electrolyzer. There is no pollution and you get to use energy that would otherwise be wasted.

More and more scientists, economists, and politicians are talking about building a new "green economy" in which green-collar jobs will replace the blue-collar jobs of displaced factory workers in polluting industries.

In West Branch, Iowa, for instance, workers now assemble wind turbines in a former pump factory.

A popular-size wind turbine in the United States stands as tall as a 30-story building and costs roughly $3.5 million to install. With good winds, this turbine can produce enough energy to meet the demand for electricity for 600 average American households—indefinitely.

No wonder the market for sustainable energy is potentially enormous. And so are the job opportunities.

Green-collar jobs cut fossil fuel emissions, lessen America's dependence on foreign oil, and curb global warming. They can also offer an exciting career and a good paycheck.

If inventing is your thing, you might come up with new ways of harvesting wind, or even new energy sources.

Coal-fired power plants, which produce half of all the electricity in the United States, release 2 billion tons of CO_2 each year. Which is why new, clean sources of energy are so important to the air.

The market for sustainable energy is potentially enormous. And so are the job opportunities.

If inventing is your thing, you might come up with new ways of harvesting wind, or even new energy sources.

Trudy Forsyth
Wind Engineer

When Trudy Forsyth traveled to Holland as a child, she became fascinated with the windmills she saw there. Now, as an engineer, she manages a project for the U.S. government that uses modern windmills, or wind turbines as they're called, to produce clean energy.

Forsyth, a former Girl Scout in Denver, Colorado, works at the National Renewable Energy Laboratory there and travels the country to explain wind energy and to promote small wind turbines.

Farmers, ranchers, and homeowners install the turbines on their property with government support. "They work best in rural areas because they are tall and you have to have quite a bit of land to put them up," she explains.

Using wind power and other non-polluting renewable energy sources plays a key part in keeping the planet from heating up too much, Forsyth says, "The more we can take the burden off the polluting energy technologies and those that require water, the healthier the planet will be."

Forsyth loves her work. "It fills my need to do something to better the planet, and at the same time I can make a great income and be in the midst of this wave of change."

After studying mechanical engineering, she worked in the aerospace industry. But the National Renewable Energy Lab was actively looking for women with advanced science degrees. Forsyth encourages girls to keep taking math and science courses "because there are going to be wonderful opportunities."

Women in engineering, Forsyth suggests, are a lot like wind energy: just getting going and poised to make an important contribution to the planet.

Meanwhile, she believes, it's important to explore every path to see where it leads. She also tried playing the clarinet and was so good at it that she studied with instructors from the Denver Symphony Orchestra and the Juilliard School of Music, played in orchestras (she still performs in a community orchestra), and almost became a professional classical musician instead of a wind-power engineer. Of course, the clarinet is also wind-powered!

Women in engineering
are a lot like wind
energy: just getting
going and poised
to make an important
contribution.

95

Mary Watkins

Lighting Up Times Square

PacWind CEO Mary Watkins grew up spending hours in the machine shop alongside her father, Phil Watkins, a machinist by trade and self-taught designer.

When Phil Watkins died in July 2008, Mary inherited the CEO mantle at PacWind, the company he formed after perfecting and patenting a unique vertical wind turbine. "It all became very clear . . . that I needed to grab the wheel and drive," Watkins says. With wind technology now the fastest-growing sector of non-petroleum energy industries, Watkins is steering her company at top speed, guided by a deep commitment to the environment.

> *Sixteen of PacWind's stackable wind turbines now alternate with solar panels to supply electricity for the first "eco-friendly" billboard in Times Square.*

PacWind turbines collect energy from winds as gentle as 5 miles per hour and as intense as 100 miles per hour. Unlike the three-blade propeller style currently used on most wind farms, vertical turbines pose no danger to wildlife. Birds and bats see them as solid objects and do not get caught in their blades.

The Wide Wind Network

More than 500 women across the United States are members of Women of Wind Energy, a networking organization for women in the wind industries. They sponsor a mentoring program for young women interested in learning about all facets of an industry that is one of the fastest growing in the world.

From the get-go, PacWind used recyclable materials and maintained a low carbon footprint. As Watkins sees it, "You can't make something with toxins that will poison the earth when you're trying to make something that's beneficial, because they cancel each other out."

Sixteen of PacWind's stackable wind turbines now alternate with 64 solar panels to supply electricity for the first "eco-friendly" billboard in New York's Times Square.

The billboard, owned by Ricoh, the global camera and technology company, represents savings of 18 tons of carbon per year. That's enough to light six houses for a year!

And, as Watkins points out, wind power "doesn't need to be mined or treated. It's native, so to speak. You can get wind from anywhere."

above the **air** *as an astronaut*

on the **air** *as a radio announcer or deejay*

AIRY
Alternatives

There are plenty of air-related jobs outside of wind energy, too.
You could be . . .

in the **air** *as a commercial airline or Air Force pilot*

air-*powered as a sailing or parasailing instructor*

studying the **air** *as an atmospheric scientist*

Wind Farm HAIKU and you

From cloud-streaked skies,
A line of silver figures
Links sloping, brown hills.

Silver bodies straight,
Faces twirl, then faces slow.
Air power their goal.
—*Kori Atazuma, 2009*

*Can you see in your mind's eye the silver figures
the poet is referring to?
What other aerial views of power do you know?*

Haiku is a Japanese verse form that has 17 syllables. In English, the haiku usually (but not always) divides the syllables like this: five in the first line; seven in the second; five in the third.

This verse form is fun to play with—and also challenging. Often the haiku begins with a nature image. Or a variation on nature. Try writing some haiku that makes use of all your senses! Let your imagination soar!

My Airy Haiku

_____

_____

_____

Miwa Koizumi
kite
Maker

Miwa Koizumi is convinced the wind blows more intensely in New York City. A world traveler, she has felt the breeze in her hair in many places. She earned master's degrees in fine art from universities in Tokyo and Paris, and now lives in the Bedford–Stuyvesant neighborhood of Brooklyn, New York. There she often scans the sidewalks for wind-blown street trash.

Koizumi is fascinated by the flight patterns of birds, insects, and random objects. When she and her partner, Marco Scoffier, spent a day videotaping soaring seagulls at Brighton Beach near Coney Island, a plastic grocery bag attracted the birds. "They thought we had food for them, and they hovered long enough for us to capture their movements in close-up." The rustling of the bag mesmerized the gulls "like white noise."

After making a video called "Flutter," Koizumi continued thinking about the swooshing noise of airborne plastic bags, which fill with breezes and lift up overhead. She began designing kites from them. "At first I thought I'd just tie a string to a bag to fly it. But it didn't go high enough," she says. Through extensive trial and error, her sturdy plastic bag kites now, as she says, take "trash to new heights" with a bamboo frame design that truly soars.

The trashbag kites by Koizumi, an artist-in-residence at various New York locations, have been adapted by kids throughout the city. They now create their own from recycled materials. In the process, they keep discarded plastic bags out of tree branches and power lines, and from blowing into sewers and waterways. Through her recycling innovations, Koizumi changes our view of ordinary throwaways and shows us a new way to fly a kite.

The first kites were made 2,800 years ago in China. Today, artists in Malaysia (above) and all over the world still create traditional kites with colorful designs.

101

BREATHE'S

LOFTY AWARD
TRACKER

Aware

GS

Your air issue is up to you and your sister Cadettes.

The Air Care Team (ACT) you mobilize will be determined by your issue.

Your approach is whatever you want to make it. The medium and the method are up to you.

Read through this tracker and fill it out as your journey takes flight. You'll find even more tips for achieving a smooth takeoff and landing on page 108.

Your air issue and approach are the basics of the AWARE, ALERT, and AFFIRM awards you can earn on this journey.

You can't go through life with your head in the clouds, even if the air is spectacular up there! Life isn't real or purposeful if you're always on cloud nine. This award is about being aware of everything going on around you on Earth. After all, you can't really care until you're aware! To earn the award:

1 Fill in your Air Log throughout your journey. Record what you see, hear, feel, and smell in your air.

2 Identify two experts who can guide you to greater air awareness and then talk to them. Who might qualify? Meteorologists, biologists, wind farm or aeronautical engineers, parasailing instructors, astronauts, physicians or other health specialists, fragrance specialists, yoga instructors. Who else can you think of?

3 Increase your AWAREness about all the issues that impact Earth's air. Hint: Check out all the air issues throughout *Breathe*. Which one grabs you most? Also, with some Cadette friends (and, of course, a trusty adult), take a walk around your school, a local business district, the local mall, or another area you think of. What air issues do you see? Think about trees (see pages 52–63) or think about noise (see pages 16–31)!

4 Now that you've sampled the air, decide on the most important, personal reason you care about Earth's air. Write a statement that explains why this reason matters to you and why it should matter to others too. Share your statement with other Cadettes. What do you learn from each other?

WHY I CARE ABOUT AIR
and
WHY OTHERS SHOULD, TOO

_____
_____
_____
_____
_____
_____
_____

Alert

The ALERT award is about alerting others. But it's also about being alert, as a member of the global community and as a leader. As you alert others, be alert to how you act as a team member. Which team skills are you great at already? Which might you improve? Alerting others is about making them aware and making them care. So be alert to how you alert! To earn the award:

1 With your Cadette team, make a collaborative choice about one air issue that you will act on together. Learn as much as you can about the topic (use some of the experts you've met) and write a statement that explains why it's important to educate and inspire others on this issue.

2 Now that you have your issue and your reasons for pursuing it, decide whom you will educate and inspire—this is your Air Care Team (ACT)! Think about it. What groups of people would be best to join with you? Principals and teachers? Parents? Your peers? Who can best assist you in moving forward?

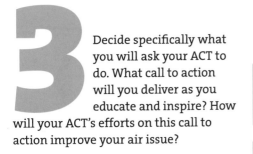

3 Decide specifically what you will ask your ACT to do. What call to action will you deliver as you educate and inspire? How will your ACT's efforts on this call to action improve your air issue?

5 Get to it! Educate and inspire! Give your Air Care Team its call to action. Feel the rewards of influencing others in a lasting way!

4 Decide *how* to reach your Air Care Team to inspire them to act on your issue. Try to engage all their senses—or at least a few of them! The medium and method are up to you. You might do something in the evening or during the school day or on a weekend. Choose a creative approach that best fits your Cadette team and your Air Care Team: a town meeting, a short play or slide show, a photo exhibit, performance art, interviews or personal stories, a booklet, or a film. Remember: If you're holding an event to get people together, think of ways for people to sustain the effort. Air needs more than just a onetime affair.

Practice Makes
Perfect

No matter what your issue or whom you will reach out to, these points are key:

• Your issue and why it matters to you

• Why it should matter to others

• What you are going to ask your Air Care Team to do to help move your issue forward toward lasting change

Be sure you can deliver these key points on demand, without hesitation.

When you're committed to educating and influencing others, you'll want to affirm what you accomplish. Affirm means to confirm! To earn this award:

Affirm

1 Follow up! What proof can you gather of progress or improvement through your efforts to educate and inspire? Contact your Air Care Team. What are they doing to benefit air? Depending on the action under way, do you have any before or after photos or other evidence? Collect and organize all responses.

2 What can you learn from the results you are hearing and seeing? Share what you learn with your Air Care Team. Want to share it further? Try contacting a local media outlet or maybe ask your library for a little space for a display of your efforts.

3 Get with your Cadette team. Maybe you're seeing some results. Maybe you hit some stumbling blocks. Either way, you've likely learned a lot. Take some time and talk it through. What will you do differently the next time you decide to act for Earth?

4 Now affirm your commitment to always strive to be a great heir for the planet.

My Airspace

_____
_____
_____
_____
_____
_____
_____
_____
_____
_____
_____
_____
_____
_____
_____
_____
_____
_____
_____
_____
_____
_____

TIPS FOR SUCCESS IN THE

AIR!

To Influence Others, Think About Yourself

Imagine that someone is about to approach you to try to gain your support for an important air issue. What methods would win you over? Most likely those methods will also win over your Air Care Team.

Make Your Message Mighty— with a Mascot

Whether an anti-smoking cowgirl or a walking tree, a mascot or spokesperson can offer a look, a personality, and a script to speak mightily about your air issue. If you create one, go all out. *Think of your mascot as your project's "brand,"* an easily identifiable and perhaps humorous way to widen your reach.

Stories
Letting Others Be Your Voice

Sometimes the best way to tell a story is with stories! Gather anecdotes and memories from community members of all ages in support of your air issue.

What changes in the air, real or desired, can further your cause?

Noticeable weather changes?

Noise or pollution changes?

Are you into video? Seek permission to film the interviews. They may become footage for an inspiring short film. Or organize them into a PowerPoint.

Remember how elephants hear with their feet? Well, butterflies taste with their feet. To see if a plant is good to eat, they just walk across it.

Chameleons can control each of their eyes separately, which means they can look up and down at the same time. That could come in handy!

And blood-hounds have a sense of smell that is 100 times better than a human being's. But bears have an even better sense of smell than bloodhounds—seven times better in fact. Bears' sense of smell is good enough to notice food from 20 miles away.

And as for a sense of touch, manatees' whole bodies are covered with tiny whiskers that help them sense all kinds of changes in the water from a distance.

What would you do if you had such heightened senses? Which would you value most?

Your Now and Future AIR

Hopefully this journey has been a breath of fresh air in your life, in more ways than one.

You've cared
for the air and seen that so much of what you enjoy in life comes to you via your senses—and comes to your senses via air!

You've also seen
that so much of what we do so senselessly to the environment gets in the air and affects everyone.

You've been claiming
your role as an heir apparent, not only of Earth's air but of all its precious resources.

So fly high with that responsibility.

To keep soaring and inspiring others to care about air, or any issue, a good leader clears the air of distractions, airs her feelings, enjoys cool breezes of inspiration, and lets her mind wander in the clouds to dream up airy—and sustainable—solutions. She engages all her senses—and the senses of others, too—to be AWARE and ALERT and AFFIRMing.

Even though your time in *Breathe* is ending, continue to breathe deep. Remind yourself now and then that even the smallest things—just one plant in one room, for example—can make a very airy difference, for you and for the planet. Clear your air whenever you can.

Clearing your air also clears your mind. That allows you to keep the air clear for everyone around you.

Clear air leaves more room for new adventures.

Look around! Airy opportunities, lofty and low-key, are nearly everywhere.

What will you, as heir apparent of Earth and all its precious resources, soar to next?

What's your favorite memory of using your senses on this journey? Did you feel more alive with all your senses consciously in play? When did you feel more AWARE, more ALERT, more AFFIRMing? When did you find yourself soaring? How did caring about air carry you to unexpected places? How did you find fresh air and fresh ideas?

In Girl Scouts,

Discover +
Connect +
Take Action
=
LEADERSHIP

What did you Discover
about your flair that can now be put
to use for the planet?

_____

_____

How can you use your inner
flair to continue to Connect with peers
and your wider community—maybe
even around the globe?

_____

_____

*If you run into turbulence,
will you use your senses
and your sense to keep a
steady course?*

*There are so many ways for
you to renew your own air and
Take Action for Earth's air—
and all of Earth's elements.*

*As Juliette
Gordon Low would
have said, keep
your windows open.
Let fresh air
into your airspace,
always.*